IMAGES OF WAR
SS PANZER DIVISIONS ON THE EASTERN FRONT

RARE PHOTOGRAPHS FROM WARTIME ARCHIVES

IMAGES OF WAR
SS PANZER DIVISIONS ON THE EASTERN FRONT
RARE PHOTOGRAPHS FROM WARTIME ARCHIVES

BOB CARRUTHERS

Pen & Sword
MILITARY

This edition published in 2018 by

Pen & Sword Military
An imprint of
Pen & Sword Books Ltd.
47 Church Street
Barnsley
South Yorkshire
S70 2AS

Copyright © Coda Publishing Ltd. 2018.
Published under licence by Pen & Sword Books Ltd.

ISBN: 9781473868403

A CIP catalogue record for this book is available from the British Library.

All rights reserved. No part of this book may be reproduced or transmitted in any form or by any means, electronic or mechanical including photocopying, recording or by any information storage and retrieval system, without permission from the Publisher in writing.

Printed and bound in England
By CPI Group (UK) Ltd., Croydon, CR0 4YY

Pen & Sword Books Ltd. incorporates the imprints of Pen & Sword Aviation, Pen & Sword Family History, Pen & Sword Maritime, Pen & Sword Military, Pen & Sword Discovery, Pen & Sword Politics, Pen & Sword Atlas, Pen & Sword Archaeology, Wharncliffe Local History, Wharncliffe True Crime, Wharncliffe Transport, Pen & Sword Select, Pen & Sword Military Classics, Leo Cooper, The Praetorian Press, Claymore Press, Remember When, Seaforth Publishing and Frontline Publishing

For a complete list of Pen & Sword titles please contact

PEN & SWORD BOOKS LIMITED
47 Church Street, Barnsley, South Yorkshire, S70 2AS, England
E-mail: enquiries@pen-and-sword.co.uk
Website: www.pen-and-sword.co.uk

INTRODUCTION

Based on the evidence of their combat record the Waffen-SS are often hailed as an elite fighting force. However, while it is true that this force fought exceptionally well in military terms, in social and humanitarian terms the reputation of the Waffen-SS, the armed political wing which grew out of the *Schutzstaffel* or Nazi party protection squads, will always be tainted by the war crimes they committed in the East and West. Their litany of crimes in the Soviet Union included the killing of those the Nazis designated as 'untermenschen' or sub humans – Slavs, Jews and Marxists.

The Waffen-SS was one of the weapons in the Nazi arsenal which was used to wage the unlooked-for war which was to lead its architects to the courtroom at Nuremberg. These men you see here were the Nazi idealists who had bought into the Nazi creed of expansion to the east in search of *Lebensraum*.

The *Lebensraum* ideology proposed an aggressive expansion of Germany and the German people. The Nazis supported territorial expansionism to gain *Lebensraum* as being a law of nature. The Nazi creed espoused the idea that it was necessary for all healthy and vigorous peoples of superior races to displace people of inferior races; especially if the people of a superior race were facing overpopulation in their given territories. The hierarchy of the Nazi Party believed that Germany inevitably needed to territorially expand because it was indeed facing an overpopulation crisis which Adolf Hitler described as follows: 'We are overpopulated and cannot feed ourselves from our own resources.' It was on this basis that expansion eastwards was justified as an inevitable necessity for Germany. From 1939 to 1941, the Nazi regime gave the outward appearance of having discarded plans to annex Soviet territories, this deceptive stance was strengthened by the improved relations with the Soviet Union via the Molotov-Ribbentrop Pact, and the public claims that central Africa was where Germany sought to achieve *Lebensraum*. Hitler publicly claimed that Germany wanted to settle the *Lebensraum* issue peacefully through diplomatic negotiations that would require other powers to make concessions to Germany; at the same time however Germany prepared for war in the cause of *Lebensraum*, and the potential clash between the peoples of Germany and the Soviet Union.

In 1941, it was the stated policy of the Nazis to kill, deport, or enslave the Polish, Ukrainian, Russian, and other Slavic populations, whom they considered inferior, and to repopulate the land with Germanic people drawn primarily from the ranks of the Waffen-SS. The urban population was considered disposable and could potentially be exterminated by starvation, thus creating an agricultural surplus to feed Germany and allowing their replacement by the population of warrior farmers who were to be rewarded with grants of land in recognition for their service in the ranks of the Waffen-SS. The policy of *Lebensraum* implicitly assumed the superiority of Germans as members of

Divisional insignia of the 1st SS Panzer Division 'Leibstandarte SS Adolf Hitler'

an Aryan master race who by virtue of their superiority had the right to displace people deemed to be part of inferior races. The Nazis insisted that *Lebensraum* needed to be developed as racially homogeneous to avoid intermixing with peoples deemed to be part of inferior races. With its strict entry requirements the Waffen-SS was the prime instrument in Hitler's vision. The man who was to give concrete form was Heinrich Himmler and it was he who was the real driving force behind the Waffen-SS in practical terms. The vague rhetoric spouted by Hitler had to be translated into practicality by Himmler. Hitler, as always had no concrete plan, as a result, those peoples deemed to be inferior races living within territory selected for *Lebensraum* were subject to arbitrary expulsion, enslavement or destruction.

Hitler gave a speech to his Waffen-SS troops just three weeks before the start of Operation Barbarossa, the Nazi code name for the attack on the Soviet Union. He said, 'This is an ideological battle and a struggle of races. Here stands a world as we conceived it – beautiful, decent, socially equal and full of culture; this is what our Germany is like. On the other side stands a population of 180,000,000, a mixture of races, whose very names are unpronounceable and whose physique is such that one can only shoot them down without mercy or compassion. When you fight over there in the east, you are carrying on the same struggle against the same sub-humanity, the same inferior races, that at one time appeared under the name of Huns, another time of Magyars, another time of Tartars, and still another time under the name of Genghis Khan and the Mongols. Today they appear as Russians under the political banner of Bolshevism.'

When he launched Operation Barbarossa Hitler expected the Wehrmacht (the German armed forces) to conquer the Soviet Union and the Waffen-SS to carry out the goals of the party. To the Wehrmacht Hitler ordered the job of 'kicking in the front door so the whole rotten Russian edifice will come tumbling down'. To the Waffen-SS therefore fell not just the job of combat but also waging a race war to create Hitler's long cherished dream of *Lebensraum*, the much-anticipated living space for the German people in the East. However, as events spiralled out of control, the war in the east became the most titanic struggle in the history of human conflict. From the opening moves the scale of the struggle was truly colossal. On one side were over three million well trained, equipped and battle hardened German troops including the Waffen-SS and half a million of their Axis allies. In total the Germans deployed 153 divisions including 21 Panzer and 14 motorised divisions containing over 3,400 tanks and 3000 aircraft. On the other side was a Soviet army of over five million men in 180 divisions with over 10,000 tanks and 20,000 aircraft.

This was a genuine life or death struggle, during operations in the East the Waffen-SS grew from just six divisions comprising 160,000 men at the start of Barbarossa until, by the end of the war, it represented a huge force of 38 combat divisions comprising over 950,000 men. Under the command of Heinrich Himmler, the Waffen-SS received privileged treatment in terms of weapons and supplies. As a consequence they attracted only the most committed recruits who were willing to fight and die for the cause. Not surprisingly with their advantages which sprang from highly motivated recruits, excellent equipment, cohesive background requirements and an all-embracing ideological indoctrination, the Waffen-SS soon earned a fearsome reputation in combat.

Divisional insignia of the 2nd SS Panzer Division 'Das Reich'

In the East Waffen-SS divisions were placed under the operational control of the *Oberkommando des Heeres* or the Supreme High Command of the Army although in practice they often acted independently. Initially the Waffen-SS was numerically insignificant when compared to regular Germany Army, however the Waffen-SS brought to Barbarossa an ideological fanaticism out of all proportion to their numbers. This sense of racial and military superiority, which was encouraged by Himmler and maintained through better pay, food and equipment, was central to the Waffen-SS philosophy. It was combined with a fanatical loyalty to Hitler, and encapsulated in the motto *'Meine Ehre heißt Treue'* or 'My honour is loyalty'. It meant that at the start of Barbarossa five of the six divisions which comprised the Waffen-SS in the field (the 'Leibstandarte Adolf Hitler', 'Das Reich', 'Totenkopf', 'Polizei' and 'Nord') were all recruited from the toughest and most ideological ethnic Germans. The exception was the 'Wiking' division, which was recruited from ideologically motivated Scandinavian, Finish, Estonian, Dutch and Belgian volunteers, but served under German officers.

German society had been indoctrinated with a sense of obedience and orders were to be followed without question. The men of the regular army had no qualms when it came to following orders; however distasteful. However, for the over-stretched regular German Army activities like racial cleansing, which did not progress their war aims, were regarded with disdain but characterised as a waste of resources rather than as a crime. From the Waffen-SS viewpoint this attitude was incomprehensible; to the men of the Waffen-SS the regular army lacked the ideology necessary to secure the final victory. The result was a severely strained relationship between the two who often disagreed on all aspects of how the campaign should be fought from the tactical to the strategic level.

The Wehrmacht launched its surprise attack on Russia at 3.15am on 22 June 1941, bombing positions in Soviet occupied Poland. Attached to the three huge army groups were the six Waffen-SS divisions. Army Group North advanced through the Baltic States and on to Leningrad, included in its ranks were 'Totenkopf', 'Polizei' and 'Nord'. Army Group Centre headed towards Moscow with 'Das Reich' in the vanguard. 'Leibstandarte' and 'Wiking' were with Army Group South and marched towards the Ukraine and Kiev.

During the first six months of Barbarossa the sheer scale of the Soviet rout in the East surprised even the German generals. On the opening day alone the *Luftwaffe* destroyed over 2000 Soviet aircraft, many on the ground and Army Group North penetrated over 50 miles into Russian territory. By the end of the first week Army Group Centre had captured Minsk and by the end of June they had advanced over 200 miles towards Moscow. By the end of September Army Group South had captured nearly half a million Soviet troops during the Battle of Kiev and Army Group North had laid siege to Leningrad. At the spearhead of all these successful advances in the East were the men of the Waffen-SS.

Yet just three months later the offensive ground to a shuddering halt. On 1 December 1941, in temperatures of minus 40 Fahrenheit, the offensive stalled at the tram terminus on the very outskirts of Moscow. Five days later the Red Army counterattacked driving the Germans back 40 miles. During Operation Typhoon or the attack on Moscow 'Das Reich' suffered catastrophic losses and of the 2000 men who had started out with the regiment in June 1941, only 35 were left alive by the end of December. While this was a crushing defeat for Germany it was to prove, in some respects at least, the making of the Waffen-SS.

By the end of 1941 the Waffen-SS had suffered over 43,000 casualties across the length of the Eastern Front. One in four Waffen-SS troops had either been killed or wounded. However, it was widely recognised, even by the Wehrmacht, that they had fought with great tenacity and without them the German army would not have got to the gates of Moscow. Eberhard von Macksensen, commander of III Army Corps in Army Group South, writing to Himmler said the 'Leibstandarte' had demonstrated 'inner discipline, cool daredevilry, cheerful enterprise, unshakeable firmness in a crisis, exemplary toughness and camaraderie'. The legend of the fanatical fighting spirit of the Waffen-SS had been born.

By the beginning of 1942, the Soviet Union was bloodied but unbowed. The changing fortunes of the campaign were reflected by the encirclement of 100,000 Germans troops from Army Group North who, in February 1942, were trapped in the Demyansk Pocket south of Leningrad. The pocket included the SS Division 'Totenkopf' who again were at the forefront of the fighting and who eventually led the breakout in April 1942. However, they paid a high price with 15,000 troops either killed or wounded. After this the Waffen-SS were never again to regain the initiative in the East but they were to fight with distinction at Kharkov and Kursk.

From 1943 to 1945, the Waffen-SS in the East were engaged in a long and bloody retreat against a numerically far superior enemy. As they fell back across the vast plains of the Soviet Union, Poland, Hungary and ultimately Germany itself, all too often their fate became death or ignominious defeat at the hands of the Red Army. But the Waffen-SS, true to their character, fought a fanatical rearguard action to the end. In the process they demonstrated what were, by objective standards, heroic, if increasingly futile, acts of bravery against overwhelming odds.

The tipping point in the East was the Soviet Union's vastly superior forces in terms of men, planes, and crucially armour, which, after 1942, began to decisively alter the outcome of the war. In order to counter the threat of the formidable Soviet T-34. The Germans had developed new tanks such as the Panther and the Tiger, but they simply could not produce them in sufficient quantities to make a difference. By the end of the war the Germans had produced nearly 6,000 Panthers and just over 1,300 Tiger tanks. In comparison the Russians were building over 1,200 T-34 tanks each month.

The devastating defeat at Stalingrad in February 1943 epitomised the changing fortunes of the Wehrmacht in the East. To counter what he interpreted as the defeatist attitude of the army, Hitler increasingly turned to the Waffen-SS whose loyalty and fighting spirit were never in question. The Wehrmacht's loss became the Waffen-SS's gain as the Führer's 'fire brigade' were used to plug the gaps and hold the line against the marauding Red Army.

By 1945, under the operational command of Heinrich Himmler, Hitler had created 38 Waffen-SS divisions and had resorted to conscripting over 900,000 men. As the situation in the East deteriorated they were drawn from an ever more diverse ethnic mix typified by the 13th Waffen-SS 'Handschar' Division which was composed of Bosnian Muslims. This unit conducted anti-partisan activities in Yugoslavia and Croatia during 1944. The result was that by the finish of the Second World War nearly half of the Waffen-SS were non-ethnic Germans despite the original strict racial requirements laid down by Himmler.

To the end Hitler possessed an almost blind faith in the fighting ability of the Waffen-SS. This was despite the fact that many of the later divisions were only regiment or brigade sized units. Furthermore the ranks were all too often filled by conscripts who lacked the experience, élan and esprit de corps of the original formations. As losses mounted the cadres from the original elite SS divisions were amalgamated to form mechanised Panzer Corps, these formations soon became the backbone of the German Army.

In March 1943, Hitler's faith in the SS Panzer Corps was rewarded. Under the charismatic leadership of Paul 'Papa' Hausser, nicknamed the father of the Waffen-SS, they pulled off a spectacular victory at Kharkov, the second largest city in the Ukraine, temporarily halting the Soviet advance. The pictures in this book bear witness to the dash they showed in the face of an overwhelming enemy.

Hausser's Panzer Corps had found themselves trapped in the city and with the defeat at Stalingrad still a fresh memory Hitler ordered them to 'stand fast and fight to the death'. Risking Hitler's wrath Hausser ignored his direct orders and instead sanctioned a strategic withdraw to prevent his tanks being decimated in the besieged city. In response Hitler flew into a blind rage and tried to sack his wayward commander. However, Hausser regrouped and without *Luftwaffe* support made a direct attack on Kharkov, eventually recapturing the city after four days of intensive, house-to-house fighting. For his bravery Hausser was awarded the Oak Leaves to his Knights Cross and officially pardoned.

Divisional insignia of the 3rd SS Panzer Division 'Totenkopf'

Others honoured with the Knights Cross, the highest award for bravery given by Nazi Germany, included Joachim Peiper, a reconnaissance commander who developed a tactic of attacking enemy-held villages by night from all sides while advancing in his armoured half-tracks at full speed, firing at every building. This tactic often set the building's straw roofs on fire and contributed to panic among enemy troops. As a result Peiper's unit gained the nickname the 'Blowtorch Battalion'.

The Battle of Kharkov was the third time the city had changed sides since the start of Operation Barbarossa, it was also to be the last victory for the Waffen-SS in the East. The offensive resulted in the Red Army suffering over 70,000 casualties, but in an ominous sign of the battles to come the SS Panzer Corps lost nearly half its combat strength.

Ironically the success of the Third Battle of Kharkov was to prove a turning point in the East not for Hitler but for Stalin because it lulled the Germans back into a false sense of their own superiority. Reinvigorated by the victory, in July 1943, Hitler sought to eliminate the Kursk salient, a bulge where the Soviet advance jutted westwards for about 80 miles into the German line. The result was Operation Citadel, the largest tank battle in history. It pitched 900,000 Germans with 2,700 tanks and 2,000 aircraft against some 1.3 million Russians with 3,600 tanks and 2,400 aircraft. Once again the Waffen-SS were in the forefront of the fighting.

The German plan was to cut off the Kursk salient by making two pincer attacks at its neck. However, unknown to the Germans the Soviets had received prior intelligence about the attack from the so called 'Lucy' spy ring based in Switzerland, acting on information provided by special operations at Bletchley Park in Oxfordshire. Stalin's commanders had therefore persuaded him to allow the Germans to attack and instead fall back to well-prepared defensive positions before counterattacking. The Waffen-SS fell into the trap.

On 5 July 1943, the northern offensive was launched and spearheaded by the SS Panzer Corps. With characteristic determination they took the attack to the enemy, and penetrated deep into the Soviet territory. When the advance eventually slowed after 22 miles of savage fighting, the Germans had destroyed over 1,149 tanks, 459 anti-tank guns, 85 aircraft and 47 artillery pieces. However, the Russians fell back on impenetrable defensive positions composed of vast minefields, innumerable field guns and supporting armour. The German offensive soon stalled and the 1st Soviet Army counterattacked inflicting large casualties on the SS Panzer Corps, forcing them into headlong retreat. The issue was decided when, a week later, six US and British divisions landed in Sicily. Fearing an imminent invasion of Italy Hitler diverted the remaining two SS Panzer Corps two thousand kilometres to the west.

The remains of the Waffen-SS in the East now found themselves constantly on the retreat. On 25 August Kharkov once again fell to the Soviets, this time for good. By the beginning of September the Germans had suffered over half a million casualties in fifty days and 1,600 tanks and assault guns had been destroyed or knocked out. Soviet casualties are not known but historians estimate the total to be twice the number of German losses. Nonetheless, for Hitler the losses were unsustainable and the Battle of Kursk proved to be the last German offensive in the East. Alexander Kovalenko, a Soviet pilot, flying over a battlefield littered with German armour declared triumphantly 'The enemy's front is broken. We are advancing.'

After Kursk morale in the army began to disintegrate but in the Waffen-SS a fanatical, if increasingly futile, fighting spirit lived on. Panzer Officer Tassilo von Bogenhardt

Divisional insignia of the 5th SS Panzer Division 'Wiking'

was typical and said after the battle 'Each German soldier considered himself superior to any single Russian, even though their numbers were so overpowering. The slow, orderly retreat did not depress us too much. We felt we were holding our own.' His illusion was rudely shattered shortly afterwards when he was badly wounded and then captured by the Soviets, the worst fate that could befall a Waffen-SS soldier.

By the end of 1943, half the territory taken by the Germans since 1941, was back under Soviet control. Russia had lost over twenty million men but they were no longer on their own. The Allies had successfully invaded Italy and, six months late, on 6 June 1944, came the D-Day landings. For the Waffen-SS this meant fighting on two fronts and more divisions being diverted from the East to the West, further weakening their ability to defend the 'Fatherland against Bolshevism'.

Even in retreat, however, the Waffen-SS proved themselves to be a formidable fighting unit. Typical of this trend was Herbert Gille, commander of the 5th SS Panzer Division 'Wiking'. In an almost suicidal move he broke out of the Korsun-Cherkassy Pocket in Northern Ukraine in 1944, against overwhelming Russian odds. For his bravery he received the Diamonds to add to his Knight Cross. Also worthy of note is *Obertsturmbannführer* or Lieutenant Colonel Leon Degrelle, commander of the 28th Waffen-SS Division 'Walloon' from Belgium. During the retreat of his division to the border of Germany in 1944, he was severely wounded but carried on fighting. As a result he was one of only three foreigners to win the Oak Leaves to the Knights Cross. He received it from Hitler's hands and later claimed Hitler told him 'If I had a son, I wish he'd resemble you.'

On May Day 1944, Stalin declared 'If we are to deliver our country and those of our allies from the danger of enslavement, we must pursue the wounded German beast and deliver the final blow to him in his own lair.' The Soviets started their pursuit on 22 June

1944, when they launched Operation Bagration, the largest and most successful offensive to be launched from Russian soil. This left the remaining Waffen-SS divisions defending a 1,000 mile front with few reserves. It was the beginning of the end.

As the war in the East moved to Poland and eventually Germany, Waffen-SS troops were among the final soldiers defending the ruins of the Reich Chancellery in Berlin. Hitler finally committed suicide on 30 April 1945, and when news of his death reached them, many of the remaining Waffen-SS troops shot themselves rather than surrender to the Soviets.

After hostilities had finally ceased on 8 May 1945, nearly one in three Waffen-SS troops were dead or missing in action. For an elite fighting force which never made up more than 10 per cent of the total German Army and had numbered just 120 men in 1933, they had fought with almost reckless courage and paid a very high price. Their mortality rate was the equivalent of all the casualties suffered by the United States military during the entire war.

The Waffen-SS had been overwhelmed by an enemy simply too strong in men and material. However, as their military situation had worsened so had their atrocities; while some non-combatant units were most obviously culpable for much of the ethnic cleansing operations, no member of the civil population could consider themselves safe from these armed ideologists. Praise for the Waffen-SS as an elite fighting force in the annals of the Second World War therefore needs to be balanced against their sinister motive and the utter ruthlessness they showed, particularly towards the Jews, Soviets and later the Poles in the suppression of the Warsaw uprising in 1944. It was here that Dr. Oskar Paul Dirlewanger commanded the infamous Waffen-SS penal unit 'Dirlewanger'. Dirlewanger was not alone and although his name is most closely linked to some of the worst crimes of the war, we can be certain that a host of similar crimes have gone unreported. Accordingly history has judged the Waffen-SS not as they would have wished – by their combat record – but instead far more ignominiously by the atrocities they carried out. When historians review the campaign in the East the fighting record of the Waffen-SS is rightly seen in the context of Hitler's ideological war against the Soviet Union. As a result there is an indelible stain on their combat record and after the war many Waffen-SS veterans were deprived of pension rights. While it is an indisputable fact that the Waffen-SS were involved in atrocities and war crimes, at the individual level there were those who fought honourably amidst the fog of war which afflicted both sides.

War crimes aside, as these pictures demonstrate, many Waffen-SS troops distinguished themselves in combat and showed incredible bravery, often against overwhelming odds. The military esteem with which the Waffen-SS were regarded can perhaps best be judged, not by their rivals in the Wehrmacht, but by their hated adversaries in the Red Army. At the victory parade in Red Square in Moscow on 24 June 1945, pride of place among the captured Nazi standards was reserved for the banner of the 1st Waffen-SS Division, the 'Leibstandarte Adolf Hitler'.

1941 – Column of Sd.Kfz. 231 (8-Rad) armoured cars of the 1st SS Panzer Division 'Leibstandarte SS Adolf Hitler' in Yugoslavia.

June 1941 – A medic checks the wounds of a reconnaissance battalion member of the 3rd SS Panzer Division Totenkopf on the Eastern Front. Two grenadiers lend a hand.

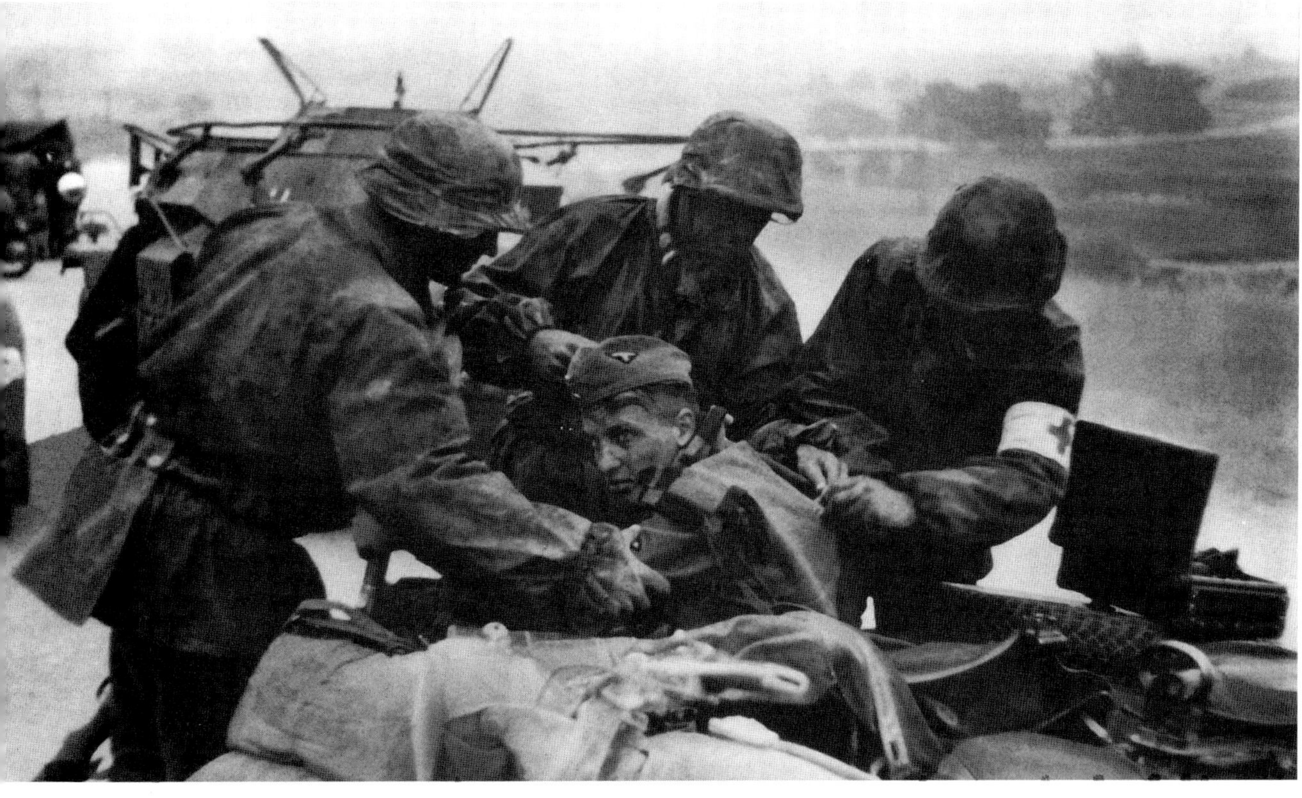

Elements of the 5th SS Panzer Division 'Wiking' look at the burning buildings left in their wake.

Red Army soldiers surrender to elements of the 1st SS Panzer Division 'Leibstandarte SS Adolf Hitler'

June 1941 – Elements of the 2nd SS Panzer Division 'Das Reich' in a Russian village during the opening weeks of the campaign. They were attached to Army Group Centre whose objective was to take Moscow. Note the 'Wolfsangel' insignia on the front right wheel arch, the symbol of the division.

Motorcycles of the 5th SS Panzer Division 'Wiking' scout ahead of the Panzers. The speed and ferocity of the German attack caught the Russians completely by surprise.

Grenadiers of the 5th SS Panzer Division 'Wiking' cover two comrades as they march a Red Army soldier into captivity.

1941 – Men of the 3rd SS Panzer Division 'Totenkopf' inspect a knocked out Russian T-26. These tanks served as the backbone of the Red Army until they were replaced by the T-34.

Forces of the 3rd SS Panzer Division 'Totenkopf' leave behind a burning Russian village in the opening weeks of Barbarossa. The division was notorious for its ethnic cleansing. It's Death's Head insignia reflected the fact that many early recruits were concentration camp guards.

1941 – A Pak 36 3.7 cm anti-tank gun belonging to the 3rd SS Panzer Division 'Totenkopf' is towed towards the front. This weapon proved of little use against the Soviet T-34 so acquired the nickname Heeresanklopfgerät, or 'tank door knocker'. It was replaced a year later by the 5 cm Pak 38.

1941 – Officers of the 3rd SS Panzer Division 'Totenkopf' attempt to navigate their way to the front in a Volkswagen Kubelwagen Type 82, the German equivalent of a jeep. Although more comfortable than a jeep, its low centre of gravity meant it struggled with the deep mud in Russia.

1941 – Norwegian motorcycle riders of the 5th SS Panzer Division 'Wiking' on the Eastern Front.

1941 – BMW R12 motorcycle of the 3rd SS Panzer Division 'Totenkopf' during the opening stages of Operation Barbarossa.

Summer 1941 – Men of the 5th SS Panzer Division 'Wiking' deployed to Russia observe the front. In the background is a Sd.Kfz. 232 reconnaissance vehicle.

Forces of the 3rd SS Panzer Division 'Totenkopf' troops crossing a makeshift bridge in a Horsh 108 troop carrier. Note the Death's Head insignia on the rear.

A reconnaissance battalion of the 5th SS Panzer Division 'Wiking'. 'Wiking' Division was recruited from Scandinavian, Finnish, Estonian, Dutch and Belgian volunteers but served under German officers.

Summer 1941 – Radio operator of the 3rd SS Panzer Division 'Totenkopf'.

Sd.Kfz. 222 Leichter Panzerspähwagen armoured car of the 2nd SS Panzer Division 'Das Reich' on the Eastern Front.

1941 – Grenadiers of the 3rd SS Panzer Division 'Totenkopf' in action during Operation Barbarossa.

June 1941 – BMW R12 motorcycle of the 2nd SS Panzer Division 'Das Reich' stuck in the mud on the Eastern Front.

1941 – Grenadiers and a Sd.Kfz 10 half-track of the 2nd SS Panzer Division 'Das Reich' advance through a Soviet village.

1941 – Kradschützen (motorcycle infantry) of the 3rd SS Division 'Totenkopf' on their way to Leningrad. Note the swastika on the side car, used for recognition by the Luftwaffe.

1941 – Grenadiers of the 1st SS Panzer Division 'Leibstandarte SS Adolf Hitler' with a Sd.Kfz. 6 fitted with a 3.7 cm FlaK 36 gun in Ukraine.

1941 – Grenadiers rush to the aid of SS-Unterscharführer Martin Bergemann of the 1st SS Panzer Division 'Leibstandarte SS Adolf Hitler' who was mortally wounded trying to destroy a Soviet T-34.

1941 – Men of the 1st SS Panzer Division 'Leibstandarte Adolf Hitler' during a break in the figthing in the Ukraine.

1941 – A column of Renault AHR 5t trucks of the 5th SS Panzer Division 'Wiking' enter the city of Zhytomyr, in the north of the western half of Ukraine. Note on the grille of the leading vehicle, a Soviet SSh-36 gas mask and a French Adrian helmet.

1941 – Grenadiers of the 5th SS Panzer Division 'Wiking' operate a MG 34 in a fire fight during Operation Barbarossa.

1941 – Elements of the 1st SS Panzer Division 'Leibstandarte SS Adolf Hitler' on the outskirts of Mariupol, Ukraine.

1941 – A reconnaissance unit of the 1st SS Panzer Division 'Leibstandarte SS Adolf Hitler' passes through a burning Russian city.

Elements of the 1st SS Panzer Division 'Leibstandarte SS Adolf Hitler' watch as a village burns. As the campaign progressed many Soviet fighters rather than surrender went into hiding and formed partisan units who operated behind German lines.

Men of the 2nd SS Panzer Division 'Das Reich' cross a river after the Soviets had blown up a bridge. The Germans attack depended upon Panzer engineers being able to quickly establish temporary pontoon bridges capable of supporting tanks.

1941 – Grenadiers of the 3rd SS Panzer Division 'Totenkopf' in action during Operation Barbarossa.

Men of the 5th SS Panzer Division 'Wiking' use a flamethrower against Soviet troops. This Model 35 flamethrower had a capacity of 2.5 gallons and a range of 25 yards. They were operated by engineers rather than combat troops and were most effective at close range against pillboxes.

August 1941 – Grenadiers of the 1st SS Panzer Division 'Leibstandarte SS Adolf Hitler' advance in Southern Russia.

August 1941 – Grenadiers of the 3rd SS Panzer Division 'Totenkopf' in the Russian town of Kingisepp.

Men of the 1st SS Panzer Division 'Leibstandarte SS Adolf Hitler' in discussion on the Russian Front.

25 August 1941 – Red Army soldiers surrender to men of the 2nd SS Panzer Division 'Das Reich'.

September 1941 – Grenadiers of the 2nd SS Panzer Division 'Das Reich' engaged in fighting in the Yelnya salient during the Battle of Smolensk.

September 1941 – Men of the 3rd SS Panzer Division 'Totenkopf' rest during a lull in the fighting. They were attached to Army Group North who advanced through the Baltic States and on to Leningrad.

September 1941 – Anti-tank unit of the 3rd SS Panzer Division 'Totenkopf'.

Panzer III tanks of the 3rd SS Panzer Division 'Totenkopf'.

1941 – SS-Sturmbannführer Walter Bestmann of the 3rd SS Panzer Division 'Totenkopf' in his Horch 901 (Kfz. 15) on the Russian Front.

1941 – A column of StuG III assault guns of the 5th SS Panzer Division 'Wiking' on the march to the Caucasus.

October 1941 – Men of the 5th SS Panzer Division 'Wiking' unload artillery brought across a river by barge.

The 2nd SS Panzer Division 'Das Reich' reached the gates of Moscow in December 1941 but the weather, massive losses and a Soviet counter offensive forced the division back.

December 1941 – Elements of the 2nd SS Panzer Division 'Das Reich' rest on the outskirts of Moscow. The division was decimated by the Soviet counter offensive and was withdrawn for rest and refitting.

From their positions 'Das Reich' forces could see the Soviet capital through their binoculars. It was the closest they would ever get. The German army would never again threaten the Russian capital.

Late 1941 – Panzer III of 5th SS Panzer Division 'Wiking' rolling towards the front near Rostov.

1942 – A parade of the 2nd SS Panzer Division 'Das Reich'. The division was decimated following Army Group Centre's failure to take Moscow and was sent to France to rest and regroup.

SS-Obersturmbannführer Hellmuth Becker (left) and SS-Hauptsturmführer Karl Adolf Ullrich (right) of the 3rd SS Panzer Division 'Totenkopf' resting in a trench after fierce fighting in the Demyansk Pocket. When the Red Army launched a counterattack in the winter of 1941/42, the 'Totenkopf' Division and several other German units were stranded in Demyansk for several months (8 February – 20 May 1942) before being freed by other German forces.

An abandoned motorcycle and sidecar of the 5th SS Panzer Division 'Wiking'. In Russian, the term 'Rasputitsa' refers to a season when travel on unpaved roads becomes difficult, owing to muddy conditions. Such conditions claimed many vehicles severely hampering the German war effort.

A MG 34 machine gun crew of the 1st SS Panzer Division 'Leibstandarte SS Adolf Hitler' in combat.

1942 – Grenadiers of the 5th SS Panzer Division 'Wiking' ride on a Panzer III. Due to continuing losses at the hands of the Soviet T-34, the Panzer III was soon superseded by the Panzer IV and the Panther.

A Tiger tank commander with the 3rd SS Divison 'Totenkopf'. The division suffered heavy casualties during the Battle of the Demyansk Pocket, but went on to fight with distinction at the Battle of Kursk.

21 June 1942 – Grenadiers and a Panzer III of the 5th SS Panzer Division 'Wiking' advance on the Eastern Front.

July 1942 – Panzer III and Panzer IV tanks of SS Panzer Regiment 5 and grenadiers of the 5th SS Panzer Division 'Wiking' entering the Russian town of Rostov.

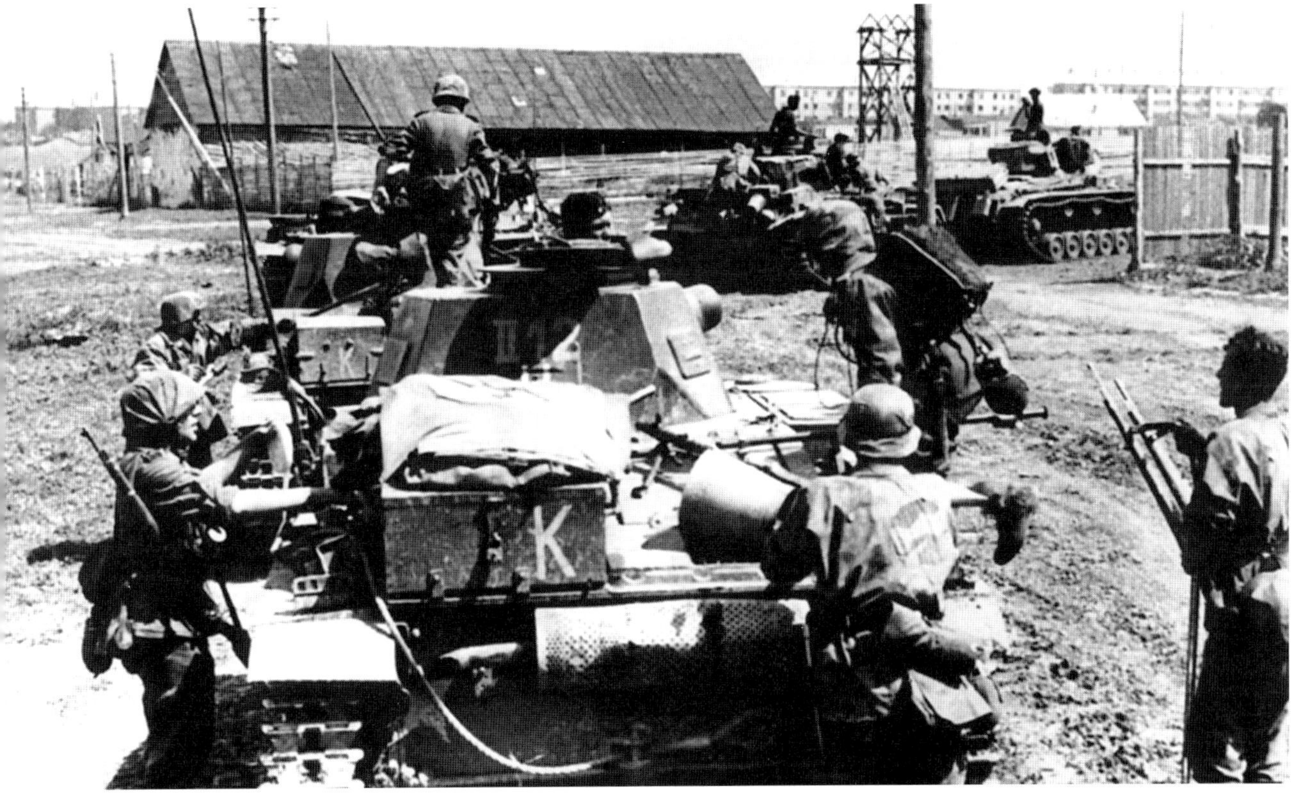

Tank men of the 5th SS Panzer Division 'Wiking' sleep beside their Panzer III.

Men of the 5th SS Panzer Division 'Wiking' repair a punctured tyre on their Opel Blitz 3.6-36S truck.

August 1942 – Inside a Panzer IV of the 5th SS Panzer Division 'Wiking' near Maykop, during the failed attempt to seize oil fields in the South Caucasus.

August 1942 – Tank commander of the 5th SS Panzer Division 'Wiking' in Maikop, Russia.

A Schwerer Panzerspähwagen (heavy armoured reconnaissance vehicle) of the 1st SS Panzer Division 'Leibstandarte SS Adolf Hitler' patrols the streets of a Russian town. This model was easy to spot because of the heavy 'bedstead' antenna over the body of the vehicle used for the short wave radio.

September 1942 – Men of the 5th SS Panzer Division 'Wiking' prior to the attack on the city of Grozny, Russia. During the fighting the division was to lose over 1,500 men and failed in its attempt to capture the city. It was to be a turning point in its campaign and the first of many setbacks.

February 1943 – Tiger of the 1st SS Panzer Division 'Leibstandarte SS Adolf Hitler' on the move in the Kharkov area.

February 1943 – Tankmen of SS Panzer Grenadier Regiment 1 of the 1st SS Panzer Division 'Leibstandarte SS Adolf Hitler' perch on the armour of a Tiger (tactical number 423) near Kharkov.

Early 1943 – Panzerbefehlswagen III with 5 cm KwK L/42 of the 3rd SS Panzer Division 'Totenkopf' on the Eastern Front.

Early 1943 – StuG III Ausf. F/8 with an extra MG 42 mounted on the fume exhaust fan. Spare track links have been fixed all around the radio box on right side. The tank was part of 3rd SS Panzer Division 'Totenkopf' during one of the phases of the Third Battle of Kharkov.

1943 – Panzer IV Ausf. G of the 1st SS Panzer Division 'Leibstandarte SS Adolf Hitler' in Kharkov.

February/March 1943 – Elements of the 1st SS Panzer Division 'Leibstandarte SS Adolf Hitler' in Kharkov.

1943 – Grenadiers of the 1st SS Panzer Division 'Leibstandarte SS Adolf Hitler' in the Kharkov area. In the background is a Sturmgeschütz III assault gun.

February 1943 – StuG III Ausf. G of the 2nd SS Panzer Division 'Das Reich' at Kharkov. This StuG, released three months earlier, in December 1942, is equipped with Winterketten and a custom-made plough for clearing snow on the road.

February 1943 – Panzer IV tanks of the 1st SS Panzer Division 'Leibstandarte SS Adolf Hitler' during the Third Battle of Kharkov. The first two tanks are outfitted with 30 mm of extra armour welded on front hull and superstructure.

March 1943 – Forces of the 3rd SS Panzer Division 'Totenkopf' in Kharkov.

March 1943 – A Tiger and its crew of the 2nd SS Panzer Division 'Das Reich' near Kharkov.

March 1943 – Grenadiers of the 1st SS Panzer Division 'Leibstandarte SS Adolf Hitler' in Kharkov.

1943 – Panzer IV of the 3rd SS Panzer Division 'Totenkopf' with grenadiers on the armour in Kharkov.

March 1943 – SS-Obersturmbannführer Kurt Meyer of the 1st SS Panzer Division 'Leibstandarte SS Adolf Hitler' during the Third Battle of Kharkov.

March 1943 – Panzergrenadiers of the 3rd SS Panzer Division 'Totenkopf' in Kharkov. This picture was taken just after the recapture of the city.

1943 – SS-Hauptsturmführer Hubert-Erwin Meierdrees of the 3rd SS Panzer Division 'Totenkopf' and SS-Obersturmbannführer Kurt Meyer of the 1st SS Panzer Division 'Leibstandarte SS Adolf Hitler' consult a map at Kharkov.

12 March 1943 – The wreckage of a destroyed Panzer IV Ausf. G of the 1st SS Panzer Division 'Leibstandarte SS Adolf Hitler' in Kharkov.

April 1943 – Tiger I of the 2nd SS Panzer Division 'Das Reich' near Kharkov, Ukraine.

May 1943 – Tiger Ausf. H1 of the 3rd SS Panzer Division 'Totenkopf' in the Russian village of Budy.

April 1943 – Tiger (tactical number 812) of the 2nd SS Panzer Division 'Das Reich'. The tank carries the nickname 'Tiki'. Below, the same vehicle can be seen with SS-Obergruppenführer Walter Kruger standing in front of the machine gun port. A Sd.Kfz. 7/1 (a Sd.Kfz. 7 half-track armed with a 2 cm Flakvierling 38 L/65 quadruple anti-aircraft gun mounting) can also be seen in the photograph.

24 April 1943 – Heinrich Himmler inspects a Tiger Ausf. E. To Himmler's left is SS-Hauptsturmführer Herbert Zimmermann, commander of the 8th company of the 2nd SS Panzer Division 'Das Reich'.

SS-Standartenführer Karl Ullrich distinguished himself in battle at Kursk. He was later the last divisional commander of the 5th SS Panzer Division 'Wiking'.

July 1943 – A Tiger of the 3rd SS Panzer Division 'Totenkopf' advances near Kursk.

1943 – Tiger Ausf. E of the 3rd SS Panzer Division 'Totenkopf' in Tver Oblast, Russia.

July 1943 – Column of StuG III Ausf. G assault guns of the 3rd SS Panzer Division 'Totenkopf' roll towards the northern part of the Kursk Salient.

July 1943 – A pair of Panzer III Ausf. M tanks, belonging to the 3rd SS Panzer Division 'Totenkopf', knocked out on the Kursk Bulge.

Summer 1943 – Tankmen of the 5th SS Panzer Division 'Wiking' load 88-mm Panzergranate 39 armour-piercing shells into a Tiger during the Battle of the Kursk.

July 1943 – Two grenadiers of the 2nd SS Panzer Division 'Das Reich' carrying a wooden board used to assist in the crossing of obstacles, pass a Tiger Ausf. E, south of Kursk Salient.

1943 – Sd.Kfz. 250/11 leichter Schützenpanzerwagen (schwere Panzerbüchse 41) of the 2nd SS Panzer Division 'Das Reich' in Ukraine.

1943 – Camouflaged machine-gun crew of the 3rd SS Panzer Division 'Totenkopf' armed with a MG 34 during the Battle of Kursk.

July 1943 – A tank crew of the 2nd SS Panzer Division 'Das Reich', pose in front of a Panzer IV near Kursk.

The commander's position in a Panther Ausf. A of the 5th SS Panzer Division 'Wiking'.

July 1943 – Tigers of 2nd SS Panzer Division 'Das Reich' advance during Operation Citadel.

Panthers of 2nd SS Panzer Division 'Das Reich' in action during Operation Citadel.

Summer 1943 – Men of the 3rd SS Panzer Division 'Totenkopf' during the Battle of Kursk.

Summer 1943 – Camouflaged Tiger of the 3rd SS Panzer Division 'Totenkopf' at Kursk.

1943 – Tankmen of the 5th SS Panzer Division 'Wiking' rest beside a Panzer III. A Sd.Kfz. 7 half-track can be seen in the background.

July 1943 – Tiger of the 3rd SS Panzer Division 'Totenkopf' at Kursk.

Panzer III of the 2nd SS Panzer Division 'Das Reich' during the Battle of Kursk.

Men of the 2nd SS Panzer Division 'Das Reich' advance with StuG III's during the Battle of Kursk.

Heavily armed grenadiers of the 2nd SS Panzer Division 'Das Reich' prior to mounting up on their Sd.Kfz. 251 half-tracks for a combined tank and infantry attack at Kursk.

July 1943 – Tanks of 3rd SS Panzer Division 'Totenkopf' press forward on the Kursk Bulge. The tank in the foreground is a Panzer III Ausf. M.

1943 – Panzer III Ausf. M and crew of the 2nd SS Panzer Division 'Das Reich' at Kursk.

1943 – An SS machine-gun crew rest in the field beside a Tiger during the Battle of Kursk. The tank belonged to the 2nd Panzer Division 'Das Reich'.

A column Tigers of the 2nd SS Panzer Division 'Das Reich' moves forward at Kursk.

Grenadiers of the 2nd SS Panzer Division 'Das Reich' supported by a Tiger I at the Battle of Kursk

1943 – StuGs of the 3rd SS Panzer Division 'Totenkopf' advance with riding infantry at Kursk.

1943 – Grenadiers of the 1st SS Panzer Division 'Leibstandarte SS Adolf Hitler' at Kursk.

July 1943 – Tiger I of the 2nd SS Panzer Division 'Das Reich' on the Kursk Bulge.

3 August 1943 – Flak-Kanoniere of the 2nd SS Panzer Division 'Das Reich' wave a flag to alert the Stuka pilots above them of their position in the region of Belgorod, Russia. The men are pictured beside a Sd.Kfz. 10/5 carrying a 2 cm FlaK 30.

Summer 1943 – Panzer III (5 cm L/60) Ausf. J Tp and Marder II of the 5th SS Panzer Division 'Wiking' on the Eastern Front.

Summer 1943 – Infantry elements of the 2nd SS Panzer Division 'Das Reich' advance during Operation Citadel. The infantryman in the foreground is carrying an MG 42.

Sd.Kfz. 251/16 Flammpanzerwagen of the 5th SS Panzer Division 'Wiking'.

1943 – Fallschirmjäger riding on a Tiger of the 2nd SS Panzer Division 'Das Reich' in Russia.

August 1943 – Panzer III Ausf. J of the 1st SS Panzer Division 'Leibstandarte SS Adolf Hitler' after the fighting at Belgorod, Russia (40 kilometres north of the border with Ukraine).

Men of the 5th SS Panzer Division 'Wiking' enjoy a smoke after some heavy fighting on the Eastern Front.

1943 – Tigers of the 1st SS Panzer Division 'Leibstandarte SS Adolf Hitler' navigate their way through the muddy terrain in the city of Vinnytsia, in west-central Ukraine

November 1943 – Men of the 1st SS Panzer Division 'Leibstandarte SS Adolf Hitler' look on helplessly as a Tiger and a truck get stuck in mud in the Fatima area of Ukraine.

30 November 1943 – Panzer IV tanks of the 5th SS Panzer Division 'Wiking' travel through snowy conditions along a road in southern Russia.

December 1943 – A column of Panzer IV Ausf. G and Tiger tanks belonging to the 2nd SS Panzer Division 'Das Reich' near the city of Kirovohrad, Ukraine.

1943 – Further struggles with the muddy conditions in Vinnytsia. Men of the 1st SS Panzer Division 'Leibstandarte SS Adolf Hitler' work to extricate a Volkswagen Type 82 Kübelwagen from the mire.

1943 – A Volkswagen Type 166 Schwimmwagen of the 1st SS Panzer Division 'Leibstandarte SS Adolf Hitler' in Ukraine. Behind the wheel is SS-Hauptsturmführer Gustav Knittel. Panthers can be seen in the backgroud.

Winter 1943 – Elements of 1st SS Panzer Division 'Leibstandarte SS Adolf Hitler' near Kharkov.

Tiger of 2nd SS Panzer 'Division Das Reich' on the Eastern Front.

February 1944 – Elements of the 5th SS Panzer Division 'Wiking' during the offensive in the Korsun-Cherkassy Pocket.

Men of the 5th SS Panzer Division 'Wiking' struggle to push a motorcycle and sidecar stuck in the mud. The soldier dressed in black is an SS-Rottenführer.

1944 – A Panther Ausf. A of the 5th SS Panzer Division 'Wiking' stuck in thick mud awaits recovery.

Medical staff of the 5th SS Panzer Division 'Wiking' attend to a seriously wounded Russian PoW. Note the large open wound on the Russian's left thigh. One of the doctors is taking the Russian's pulse.

January/February 1944 – Men of the 1st SS Panzer Division 'Leibstandarte SS Adolf Hitler' during the Battle of the Korsun-Cherkassy Pocket.

April 1944 – SS-Untersturmführer Helmut Becker of the 3rd SS Panzer Division 'Totenkopf' reading a telegram with a Heer Oberleutnant from Sturmgeschütz-Brigade 228 in front the wreckage of a Soviet T-34, in Romania.

1944 – The same men of the 3rd SS Division 'Totenkopf' break for a meal beside the destroyed T-34.

6 April 1944 – Panzer-Befehlswagen V (7.5 cm Kw.K. L / 70) Panther Ausf. A (Sd.Kfz 267 or 268) in the Kovel Pocket. The vehicle was commanded by SS-Standartenführer Johannes Mühlenkamp of SS Panzer Regiment 5 of the 5th SS Panzer Division 'Wiking'. The infantry in the foreground are from the regular 131st Infantry Division. They are heavily armed with the MG-42, MP-43, and Panzerfausts.

Spring 1944 – Panther of the 5th SS Panzer Division 'Wiking' in the Kovel sector.

27 April 27 1944 – A soldier of the 5th SS Panzer Division 'Wiking' speaking through a Feldfernsprecher 33 (FF33) field telephone. In the background, Panthers belonging to the 5th SS Panzer Division 'Wiking' move forward. The photo was most probably taken south of Kovel.

Panther Commander of of the 5th SS Panzer Division 'Wiking'.

5th Company of the 5th SS Panzer Division 'Wiking' during a brief halt in the fighting.

Summer 1944 – Officers of the 5th SS Panzer Division 'Wiking' pictured on the engine deck of a Panther in Russia.

SS-Obersturmführer Karl Nicolussi-Leck, Commander of the 8th Company of SS Panzer Regiment 5, of the 5th SS Panzer Division 'Wiking', receives the Knight's Cross.

1944 – Panther and Sd.Kfz. 251 half-track with crews on a road in the suburbs of Warsaw. Second from the left of the tank is Karl Nicolussi-Leck.

SS-Obersturmführer Karl Nicolussi-Leck's Panther of the 5th SS Panzer Division 'Wiking'.

June 1944 – Elements of the 5th SS Panzer Division 'Wiking' in Pomerania (south-east of Warsaw).

June 1944 – Panther Ausf. A and SdKfz 251/7 of the 5th SS Panzer Division 'Wiking' in Pomerania.

Summer 1944 – Panzer IV Ausf. H of the 3rd SS Panzer Division 'Totenkopf'.

1944 – Grenadiers of the 5th SS Panzer Division 'Wiking' advance beside a Panther Ausf. A in Poland.

The Panzer IV was in service until 1945. This tank served with the 3rd SS Panzer Division 'Totenkopf'.

June 1944 – A command Panther of the 5th SS Panzer Division 'Wiking' lies abandoned having been knocked out during the drive to Kovel.

1944 – The crew of a Tiger Ausf. E (tactical number 901) rest on the armour of their tank. The men belonged to the 9th company of SS Panzer Regiment 3 of the 3rd SS Panzer Division 'Totenkopf'.

1944 – Men of the 3rd SS Panzer Division 'Totenkopf' work together to dismantle the tower of a Tiger in a Polish forest.

An assault group of the 5th SS Panzer Division 'Wiking' moves up along a railway embankment to relieve the Kovel Pocket.

1944 – Grenadiers of the 5th SS Panzer Division 'Wiking' during the attempted exit from the Korsun–Cherkasy Pocket.

July 1944 – Personnel and equipment of the 5th SS Panzer Division 'Wiking' near the Polish village of Matseevo. In the foreground is a Volkswagen Type 166 Schwimmwagen. In the background is a Sd.Kfz. 251 half-track and a Panther (tactical number 501).

July 1944 – Panthers of the 3rd SS Panzer Division 'Totenkopf' during the retreat into Poland.

Panthers of the 5th SS Panzer Division 'Wiking' in action during the fighting east of Warsaw.

Summer 1944 – Panthers of the 5th SS Panzer Division 'Wiking' viewed through a S.F.14. Z. Gi stereo binocular in Eastern Poland. Infantry is hidden under the slope of the road.

Summer 1944 – Untersturmführer Gerhard Mahn, commander of 11th company, SS Panzer Grenadier Regiment 9 'Germania' of the 5th SS Panzer Division 'Wiking' directs the action east of Warsaw

July 1944 – In the Żerczyce area, Poland, officers of the 5th SS Panzer Division 'Wiking' confer. Hans-Georg Jessen (left), the commander of a company in SS Panzer Regiment 5, talks with Friedrich Hannes, the commander of an armoured company of SS Panzer Grenadier Regiment 9 'Germania'.

Jessen was one of the first officers assigned to the Division's tank battalion in 1942. Only 25 years old at the time, he was awarded German Cross in Gold on 15 December 1943 for leading the Division's Sturmgeschütz battery in the course of the the retreat to the Dnieper River during the previous autumn.

13 July 1944 – Panther tanks of the 5th SS Panzer Division 'Wiking' at the railway station in Liuboml, Ukraine, during the relocation from Kovel to the area of the Białowieża, Poland.

22 July 1944 – Panther (tactical number 534) of the Mühlenkamp Combat Group of the 5th SS Panzer Division 'Wiking' in the Nurzec-Stacja area.

22 July 1944 – Standartenführer Johannes-Rudolf Mühlenkamp, Commander of the 5th SS Panzer Division 'Wiking', pictured in front of a Befehlspanzer Panther.

22 July 1944 – Men of SS Panzer Grenadier Regiment 9 'Germania', SS Panzer Regiment 5, of the 5th SS Panzer Division 'Wiking' in Sd.Kfz. 251/1 Ausf. D armoured personnel carriers in front of the counterattack, in the Nurzec–Stacja area. A 8.8 cm Raketenpanzerbüchse 43, or 'Ofenrohr' (stovepipe) hand-held anti-tank grenade launcher is attached to the armour of the Sd.Kfz. 251/1.

22 July 1944 – Officers of the Kampfgruppe Mühlenkamp of the 5th SS Panzer Division 'Wiking' in a Sd.Kfz. 251/3 Ausf. D armoured personnel carrier during the fighting in the village of Wilanów, Poland.

22 July 1944 – Personnel and equipment of the Kampfgruppe Mühlenkamp during the fighting at Wilanów. A Sd.Kfz. 251 half-track advances beside a Panther (tactical number 533).

July 1944 – SS-Standartenführer Johannes-Rudolf Mühlenkamp places a stick grenade into the barrell of the 76 mm main armament of a disabled Soviet SU-76M.

July 1944 – A column of the 5th SS Panzer Division 'Wiking' move along a village street in eastern Poland. In the forground, soldiers move in a Sd.Kfz. 251 half-track. In the background, Panther tanks.

July 1944 – Officers of the 5th SS Panzer Division 'Wiking' in a Sd.Kfz. 251 half-track during the fighting in Eastern Poland. The armoured personnel carrier moves in the column behind a Panther.

July/August 1944 – Sd.Kfz. 251/2 Ausf. D of the 5th SS Panzer Division 'Wiking' with an 8 cm Granatwerfer 34/1 in Poland.

August 1944 – Panther tanks of the 5th SS Panzer Division 'Wiking' on the Eastern Front. Panthers played a decisive part in the successful breakout from the Korsun-Tscherkassy Pocket.

1944 – A Befehlspanzer Panther from the SS Panzer Regiment 5 of the 5th SS Panzer Division 'Wiking' on the Eastern Front.

1944 – Panther Ausf. A (tactical number 501) under the command of SS-Untersturmführer Norbert Neven du Mont of the 5th SS Panzer Division 'Wiking' in combat.

Men of the 5th SS Panzer Division 'Wiking' in combat positions.

Autumn 1944 – Grenadiers of the 5th SS Panzer Division 'Wiking' advance behind a Panther in Poland.

1944 – Hanomag half-track of the 5th SS Panzer Division 'Wiking' outside Warsaw.

1944 – Panther (tactical number 613) of the 5th SS Panzer Division 'Wiking' in Ukraine.

August 1944 – Grenadiers of the 3rd SS Panzer Division 'Totenkopf' near Iasi, in Eastern Romania.

October 1944 – A grenadier of the 3rd SS Panzer Division 'Totenkopf' talking with a Hungarian soldier in Budapest. The Tiger II in the background is from the 503rd Heavy Panzer Battalion.

Winter 1944 – The view from the turret of a Panther of the 5th SS Panzer Division 'Wiking' on the railway embankment to Kovel.

Winter 1944/1945 – Soviet soldiers inspect a pair of captured Tigers belonging to the 1st SS Panzer Division 'Leibstandarte SS Adolf Hitler.'

January 1945 – A road strewn with debris must be cleared so that the semi-tracks of the 3rd SS Panzer Division 'Totenkopf' can progress between Bajót and Bajna in Hungary during Operation Konrad.

5 January 1945 – A Sturmgeschütz 7.5 cm Stu.K. 40 Ausf. G mit Seitenschürzen (Sd.Kfz 142/1), with a winter camouflage wash over a layer of Zimmerit, rolls through the Hungarian village of Szomor (west of Budapest) during 'Operation Konrad I'. Onboard are grenadiers of the 3rd SS Panzer Division 'Totenkopf'.

20 January 1945 – Men of the 3rd SS Panzer Division 'Totenkopf' during Operation Konrad at Szomor.

1945 – A Panzer IV of the 3rd SS Panzer Division 'Totenkopf' passes by a wrecked T-34 in Hungary.

1945 – Panthers of the 3rd SS Panzer Division 'Totenkopf' roll forward through Hungary.

March 1945 – Panther Ausf. G of the 3rd Panzer Division SS 'Totenkopf' knocked out in the Hungarian village of Magyaralmás. The number of the Soviet trophy team can be seen on the tower of the tank.

Knocked out Tiger of the 3rd SS Panzer Division 'Totenkopf' in the Lake Balaton area. The Soviet team '308 A' captured the tank.